To

Olivia

From

Aunt Dawn

Written and compiled by Sophie Piper
Illustrations copyright © 2012 Melanie
Mitchell
This edition copyright © 2012 Lion Hudson

The moral rights of the author and illustrator
have been asserted

A Lion Children's Book
an imprint of
Lion Hudson plc
Wilkinson House, Jordan Hill Road,
Oxford OX2 8DR, England
www.lionhudson.com
ISBN 978 0 7459 6287 0

First edition 2012
10 9 8 7 6 5 4 3 2 1 0

Acknowledgments
Every effort has been made to trace and
contact copyright owners for material used in
this book. We apologize for any inadvertent
omissions or errors.

All unattributed prayers are by Sophie Piper
and Lois Rock, copyright © Lion Hudson.
Bible extracts are taken or adapted from the
Good News Bible published by the Bible
Societies and HarperCollins Publishers, ©
American Bible Society 1994, used with
permission.

The Lord's Prayer (on page 20) as it appears
in *Common Worship: Services and Prayers for the
Church of England* (Church House Publishing,
2000) is copyright © The English Language
Liturgical Consultation and is reproduced by
permission of the publisher.

A catalogue record for this book is available
from the British Library

Typeset in 15/20 Baskerville Regular
Printed in China January 2012
(manufacturer LH17)

Distributed by:
UK: Marston Book Services Ltd,
PO Box 269, Abingdon, Oxon OX14 4YN
USA: Trafalgar Square Publishing,
814 N Franklin Street, Chicago, IL 60610
USA Christian Market: Kregel Publications,
PO Box 2607, Grand Rapids, MI 49501

First Prayers with Jesus

Sophie Piper

Illustrated by Melanie Mitchell

LION
CHILDREN'S

Contents

The shepherds found Jesus wrapped in swaddling clothes and cradled in a manger.

The song of Christmas angels
Rings out from year to year;
Jesus, born so long ago,
Still gathers with us here.
We listen to his stories,
We learn to say his prayer,
We follow in his footsteps
And learn to love and share.

Jesus said, "Let the children come to me and do not stop them, because the kingdom of God belongs to such as these."

Jesus, friend of little children,
Be a friend to me;
Take my hand, and ever keep me
Close to thee.

Walter J. Mathams (1851–1931)

11

Jesus said, "The kingdom of God is like a seed that grows."

The kingdom of God
is like a tree
growing through
all eternity.

In its branches,
birds may nest;
in its shade,
we all may rest.

Jesus said, "Let your life shine with good deeds.
Then you will be light for the world."

Jesus bids us shine,
With a pure, clear light,
Like a little candle,
Burning in the night.
In this world of darkness,
So let us shine –
You in your small corner,
And I in mine.

Susan Warner (1819–1885)

Jesus said, "It is easy to love your friends; remember also to love your enemies."

The sun may shine,
the rain may fall:
God will always
love us all.

We too must
love everyone
in wind and rain
and golden sun.

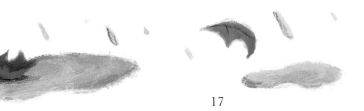

Jesus said, "When you pray, go to your room, close the door, and pray to your Father, who is unseen."

Here I am where no one sees
and all alone in prayer;
but I know God is listening,
for God is everywhere.

*Jesus said, "When you pray, do not use a lot of words.
Your Father already knows what you need. This, then,
is how you should pray."*

Our Father in heaven,
hallowed by your name,
your kingdom come,
your will be done,
on earth as in heaven.
Give us today our daily bread.
Forgive us our sins
as we forgive those who sin against us.
Lead us not into temptation
but deliver us from evil.

The prayer Jesus taught

For the kingdom, the power,
and the glory are yours
now and for ever.
Amen.

A traditional ending

*Jesus said, "If you know you have made mistakes, speak
to God humbly and truthfully, and God will forgive you."*

Deeply sorry,
deeply sad;
things I did
were deeply bad.

Deeply hoping
God above
will enfold me
in his love.

Jesus said, "If you forgive others the wrongs they have done to you, your Father in heaven will also forgive you."

From the earth
a golden harvest

From the storm
a clear blue sky

As we pardon
one another

God forgives us
from on high.

Jesus said, "Make it your aim to live as God wants, and God will take care of all you need."

God feeds the birds that sing from
   the treetops;
God feeds the birds that wade by the sea;
God feeds the birds that dart through
   the meadows;
So will God take care of me?

God clothes the flowers that bloom on
the hillside;
God clothes the blossom that hangs from
the tree;
As God cares so much for the birds and
the flowers
I know God will take care of me.

Jesus said, "Your Father in heaven will give good things to those who ask him."

Dear Father God in heaven,
Please hear my asking prayer;
For Jesus said I will receive
Your blessings everywhere.

Dear Father God in heaven,
I'm seeking for the way;
And Jesus said that you will guide me
Each and every day.

Dear Father God in heaven,
I'm knocking at your door;
For Jesus said you'll let me stay
Beside you evermore.

Jesus said, "Do for others what you want them to do for you."

Little deeds of kindness,
Little words of love,
Help to make earth happy,
Like the heaven above.

Julia Carney (1823–1908)

Jesus said, "Choose the narrow gate: the one that leads to life."

I will choose the narrow path,
I will walk the straight,
Through the wide and winding world
Up to heaven's gate.

Jesus said, "Love God and one another: that is the great commandment."

Love the Lord with all your strength,
with heart and soul and mind;
and love your neighbour as yourself
and be for ever kind.

Jesus said, "Say only the things you would not be ashamed for God to hear."

Words can make us happy
Words can make us sad
Words can help us all be friends
WORDS CAN MAKE US MAD!
So we must be careful
In the things we say
Dear God, help us choose the words
That we use today.

Jesus said, "I am the good shepherd."

Loving Shepherd of Thy sheep,
Keep Thy lambs, in safety keep;
Nothing can Thy power withstand;
None can pluck us from Thy hand.

Jane Eliza Leeson (1807–82)

Look! God's chosen king is coming.
He is humble and is riding on a donkey.

Let's sing and clap and wave and cheer
for Jesus, who comes riding near.

Let's cheer and wave and clap and sing
to welcome Jesus as our king.

Jesus said, "I am giving you a new commandment:
love one another.
As I have loved you, so you must love
one another."

Love is giving, not taking,
mending, not breaking,
trusting, believing,
never deceiving,
patiently bearing
and faithfully sharing
each joy, every sorrow,
today and tomorrow.

Jesus said, "There are many rooms in my Father's house, and I am going to prepare a place for you.
"I am the way, the truth, and the life."

The winter branches were bare and grey
But now the blossom is white;
For Jesus was hung on a tree to die
But God has put all things right.

The way to heaven was blocked and barred
But now it lies open wide;
And all of God's children may enter in
With Jesus, their friend and guide.

Lord Jesus' grace
to everyone
from dawn
until the setting sun;

to all throughout
the long dark night;
to bring us safe
to morning's light.